Write On...

ENDANGERED ANIMALS

Clare Hibbert

W

FRANKLIN WATTS

LONDON • SYDNEY

Franklin Watts
Published in Great Britain in paperback in 2018
by The Watts Publishing Group

Copyright © The Watts Publishing Group, 2016

Credits
Series Editor: Melanie Palmer
Conceived and produced by Hollow Pond
Editor: Clare Hibbert @ Hollow Pond
Designer: Amy McSimpson @ Hollow Pond
Illustrations: Kate Sheppard
Photographs: Alamy: 5 (Carver Mostardi), 6-7 (Bruce Corbett),
9 (Ivan Kuzmin), 11 (Martin Harvey), 14-15 (imageBROKER),
17 (Rob Crandall), 19 (Edo Schmidt), 26-27 (Steffen Binke); Shutterstock: cover
(leungchopan), 13 (Gudkov Andrey), 20-21 (Matt Elliott), 23 (Daniel Precht),
25 (Hung Chung Chih), 29 background (ozgun evren erturk), 29br (Matt Knoth).
Every attempt has been made to clear copyright. Should there be any inadvertent
omission please apply to the publisher for rectification.

ISBN 978 1 4451 5009 3

Printed in China

FSC
www.fsc.org
MIX
Paper from
responsible sources
FSC® C104740

Franklin Watts
An imprint of
Hachette Children's Group
Part of The Watts Publishing Group
Carmelite House
50 Victoria Embankment
London EC4Y 0DZ

An Hachette UK Company
www.hachette.co.uk
www.franklinwatts.co.uk

You can help to save endangered animals. Raise some money and donate it to an organisation such as WWF (their website address is on page 31).

Look out for the **Write On...** writing tips and tools scattered through the book, then head to the Writing school on page 28 for project ideas to inspire your awesome inner author.

Write On...
ENDANGERED ANIMALS

CONTENTS

Who's endangered?

Around the world, all kinds of animals are disappearing from the wild – from tiny insects to large mammals. An animal that has disappeared forever is called extinct. Animals that are in danger of becoming extinct are called endangered.

Until people began travelling and exploring, no one had any idea how many different kinds of animal there were in the world! Today, we have built up a good picture of the animal kingdom. Scientists can count or estimate how many of each species there are.

Saving wildlife

It's worrying when scientists notice animal numbers falling. Once a species is extinct, it is gone forever. We should do whatever we can to save wildlife for future generations to enjoy.

Scientists are still finding new species! Nearly 50 new snails were discovered in 2015, including a record-breakingly small one, just 0.7 mm tall.

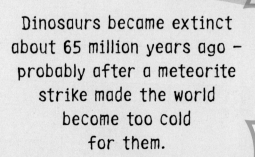

Dinosaurs became extinct about 65 million years ago – probably after a meteorite strike made the world become too cold for them.

4

Hundreds of insects are endangered, including this glasswing butterfly.

Write On...

When you're writing, use punctuation for emphasis. A dash can add drama – and don't forget exclamation marks! Can you find examples of both on these two pages?

Going, going, gone!

It's unusual for a species to disappear overnight. Usually its numbers slowly fall. The Red List is an official list that keeps track of the numbers of wild animals and says how in danger they are.

If an animal looks as if it could be in trouble soon, the Red List calls it Near Threatened (NT). If it's already under threat, it is Vulnerable (VU). Then come Endangered (EN) and Critically Endangered (CR). After that, the species dies out and becomes extinct.

Two types of 'extinct'

Some animals have disappeared in nature but still survive in zoos or breeding centres. They are Extinct in the Wild (EW). Others don't even exist in captivity. They are well and truly Extinct (EX).

The scimitar oryx is found in zoos but it is extinct in the wild.

Every species on the Red List is given two letters that show how much trouble it's in. The letters EN mean an animal is endangered.

Some animals disappear but their relatives live on. Elephants belong to the same family as extinct woolly mammoths.

Write On...

Use real facts and news as inspiration. In 2015, scientists put DNA from a woolly mammoth into elephant cells. Write a story set in a future where mammoths roam the earth again!

Different dangers

Animals don't all become endangered
for the same reasons. Sometimes their
numbers fall because of things that people
do. Other times, animals can't adapt to
changes brought about by natural causes.

 People may hunt animals
to extinction.

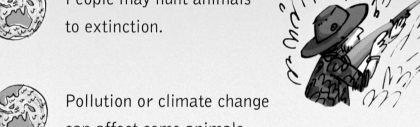

 Pollution or climate change
can affect some animals.

 People may bring
new animals to a
place, and they
eat the existing
animals.

 Disease can wipe out an
animal population.

One of the main threats to
animals is their homeland
disappearing. This is called
habitat loss.

The dodo died out within 25 years
of people (and their pet cats
and dogs) settling on its
home island, Mauritius.

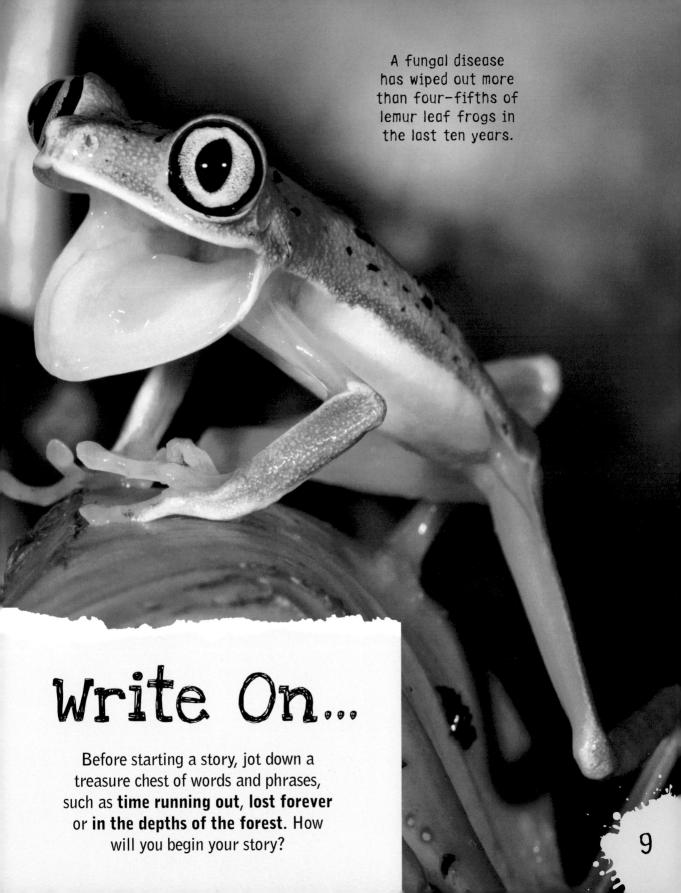

A fungal disease has wiped out more than four-fifths of lemur leaf frogs in the last ten years.

Write On...

Before starting a story, jot down a treasure chest of words and phrases, such as **time running out**, **lost forever** or **in the depths of the forest**. How will you begin your story?

Less space to live

In many parts of the world, the wild places where animals live – their habitats – are disappearing. Animals don't have as much space to feed and raise their young. This puts them in danger of dying out.

People are the main cause of habitat loss. We clear the land for farmland for crops or animals. In some places we dig mines. We also use land to build towns, cities or holiday resorts.

Lost homes

Rainforests are just one of the habitats that are disappearing. When they are changed or destroyed, there is nowhere for all the animals that once lived there to go. They can no longer survive.

As habitats disappear, animals end up stranded. Pandas get stuck with no bamboo to eat!

To protect the white rhino, people have created 'wildlife 'corridors' – strips of land that link wild areas. Rhinos can reach new territories – and mates!

This lemur, a crowned sifaka, is endangered because people are cutting down the Madagascan forests where it lives.

Write On...

Try your hand at a news story about animals losing their homes. Keep your sentences short, punchy and full of facts.

Changing world

Our world is becoming hotter. This is called global warming. 'Greenhouse gases' are making Earth's atmosphere trap more heat from the Sun. The gases are released when we burn fossil fuels such as petrol, coal and wood.

Global warming is affecting our climate – the planet's average weather patterns. It is causing more droughts in hot places, and affecting the seasons in cooler places. Animals that migrate may arrive at their feeding grounds too late for the plants or animals that they usually eat.

Melting ice caps

Ice melting at the poles means polar animals are losing their homes. The melted ice is also making sea levels rise – and that spells trouble for animals such as turtles that lay their eggs on beaches. It affects animals in low-lying coastal areas, too. Their habitats are simply being washed away.

If spring comes early, insects breed earlier. When swallows and other migrating birds arrive, the juicy caterpillars have already changed into butterflies. The birds go hungry, and their numbers fall.

Icebergs and ice floes (sheets of floating ice) are melting. There are fewer resting places now for polar bears.

Write On...

Write a poem about polar animals in danger. If you want it to rhyme, try words such as **floe** and **go** or **bear** and **nowhere**. You could use a rhyming dictionary to help you.

Climate change is the biggest threat to polar bears.

Loss of food

Some animals are endangered because they don't have enough food to eat to survive. There can be different reasons for this. The main ones are climate change and competition from other animals or from people.

Climate change can turn grassland into desert. That means no food for grazing animals, or the predators that hunt them. Climate change is also warming the oceans. That means fewer cool-water animals, such as shrimp-like krill, and fewer krill-eaters, such as whales.

Overfishing

One example of competition is when people catch lots of fish. There are fewer fish in the sea for sharks and other marine predators.

Overfishing by people means less fish for the endangered hammerhead shark.

When people hunt animals such as deer to eat, there aren't so many left for wolves, big cats and other predators.

Krill is not just affected by climate change. People are harvesting lots of it to put into health supplements.

Write On...

Write about a hammerhead shark searching for a meal. Now try it in the first person, as if you are the shark. Which has the most impact?

Food and medicines

Some animals are hunted and killed by people for food or medicines. If people take too many, the animals become endangered. It is illegal to hunt or kill endangered animals, but some people do it anyway. They are called poachers.

 Chinese alligators are hunted for their meat. People think it cures colds.

 Some people eat bushmeat – meat from wild rainforest animals, including endangered chimps, pygmy hippos and tapirs.

 Tiger bones, claws and teeth are used in medicines.

 Endangered shark species are killed when their fins are taken for shark's fin soup. The dish is a delicacy in China.

Many other animals are killed for use in traditional medicines. Rhino and water buffalo horns are supposed to stop fevers.

Write On...

An onomatopoeia (say *o-no-mat-oh-pee-a*) is a word that sounds like its meaning – great for atmospheric sound effects! Try **snap**, **rustle** and **crack** if your story's about poachers pursuing a tiger.

White rhinos are threatened. Hunters want their horns for medicines and weapons.

Furs and skins

In the past, many animals were hunted for their skins. It is now illegal to sell fur or skin from endangered animals, but the trade still happens because the sellers can make a lot of money.

During the 1800s, fur seals were almost hunted to extinction. Then laws were made to protect them and populations began to recover.

Many cats are killed for their fine fur. People prize the spotted coats of jaguars, margays and ocelots and striped coats of tigers. South America's giant otters nearly disappeared because their velvety pelts sold for such high prices.

The leather trade

People also want to buy the patterned hides of okapi, zebras and giraffes. Crocodiles and snakes are killed for their skins, too, which make textured leather for bags, belts and shoes.

There are campaigns to stop people wearing fur. One involved throwing cans of blood-red paint over fur coats.

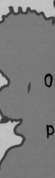

RED PAINT

The clouded leopard is hunted for its fur. Its forest habitat is also being destroyed.

Write On...

Write a leaflet to save a critically endangered animal. Think about five key points to support your argument.

Hunted down

Hunting is not always about a meal on the table or fur for a coat. Some people just hunt for the fun of it. It is hard for animal-lovers to understand, especially when the hunted animals are endangered.

Hunters enjoy showing off their skill with a shotgun or other weapon. They also find it exciting to be near a dangerous animal. They usually keep part of the kill as a prize or trophy.

Helpful hunting?

Many people believe it is wrong to hunt endangered animals. However, a few people argue that hunting can help. They say that hunters pay a lot of money to buy their licence to hunt, and that money can be used to conserve land for endangered species.

Grey wolves are endangered but they are still hunted. People fear the wolves and don't want their numbers to rise.

People still go on safari holidays to Africa to shoot animals. The prized "big five" are the elephant, lion, leopard, white rhino and Cape buffalo.

African elephants have already been hunted to extinction in some countries where they once lived.

Write On...

An adverb is a word that describes an action. In **The hunter aimed his rifle carefully.**, the adverb is **carefully.** Can you think of more adverbs?

Wild pets

Some animals are taken from the wild to become pets. Others are captured and sold to private zoos. This is bad news for any wild animal, but especially for endangered ones, whose numbers are already falling.

Taking animals from the wild can affect their habitats. It upsets the natural balance of plants, plant-eaters and predators.

Parrots, macaws and other rare and beautiful birds are popular as pets. So are exotic fish, frogs and reptiles, monkeys and chimps. It's illegal to trade in endangered animals, but breeders and collectors will pay high prices.

Caged

Many animals suffer and die on the way to their new homes, because they are transported in cramped, dirty cages. If they survive, they face a life in captivity, away from their natural habitat.

Cute baby chimps grow into aggressive adults. It can't be much fun for them to live out their days on their own in a cage.

Write On...

Imagine writing a story about a stolen animal being rescued. What tense will you use? Present tense will make it feel more immediate and 'now'. Past tense might add drama.

In the past, many wild
hyacinth macaws were
taken for the pet trade.
Today the birds are
classed as vulnerable.

Breeding programmes

One way of helping endangered animals is to try and breed them in captivity. Later, perhaps, they can be introduced back into the wild – so long as their habitat is still there and safe for them.

 Many zoos have breeding programmes. They encourage their own animals to mate, or invite animals from other zoos.

 Inbreeding (when close relatives mate) means offspring have more risk of health problems. To stop this, breeding centres keep 'family trees' of their animals.

Animals can be studied closely in zoos and breeding centres. Findings about captive pandas are helping their wild cousins.

Not all captive-born animals can be released. Some become so used to being fed that they lose their hunting instinct.

These panda cubs were born at Chengdu, a breeding and research centre in southwest China.

Write On...

In any short story, it's good to have a 'turning point' – a moment when the plot changes direction. Try a zoo story where all the animals escape!

Reserves

Habitat loss is one of the biggest threats to endangered animals, so one of the best ways to help them is by creating reserves. A reserve is an area that is protected. It can be on land or in the sea.

Sometimes land being protected simply means that the place must stay wild – no homes or businesses can be built there, for example. But some reserves have to be physically protected – they need armed guards on patrol to stop poachers taking animals or plants.

Saving animals

People who work on reserves care about endangered animals. So do many other people around the world. They join conservation groups that raise awareness and encourage governments to act. Some groups even buy land and create their own safe wildlife reserves.

The Great Limpopo reserve is Africa's biggest reserve, covering nearly 100,000 sq km. Part of it was made into a national park as long ago as 1898!

An endangered green turtle swims through the Great Barrier Reef Marine Park.

NO FISHING

Australia's Great Barrier Reef has been protected since 1975.

Write On...

Paint a picture with words! Describe the scene in lots of detail. For example, a diver at a reef might see **colonies of colourful coral, anemones waving deadly tentacles, darting clownfish** and **lurking moray eels**.

Write On... Writing school

Are you ready to show off some of the terrific endangered animal facts you've found out? First, decide on your form. Here are some ideas:

 A campaign poster trying to stop habitat loss

 A diary by a tour guide taking people up the Amazon river

 A short story about raising an orphaned panda

 A blog by someone horrible, boasting about going on a big-game hunt

 If you like drawing, put across an important message through a comic strip, like the one below about pet parrots.

SOME MACAWS ARE STILL TAKEN FROM THE WILD TO BE SOLD AS PETS, EVEN THOUGH IT'S ILLEGAL.

ALWAYS CHECK WHERE A BIRD HAS COME FROM. ASK THE PET SHOP OWNER BEFORE YOU BUY.

RESPONSIBLE SHOPS SELL PETS THAT HAVE BEEN BRED IN CAPTIVITY, NOT TAKEN FROM THE WILD.

A news story needs a snappy headline to attract the reader's attention, followed by a short paragraph that outlines the most important points. Then the main story goes into all the details.

See if you can find a picture online or in a magazine to illustrate your news article.

CONDOR FACT FILE

• The California condor is North America's biggest bird, with a 3-m wingspan.

• The total condor population (captive and wild) is around 425 birds.

• A condor's average lifespan is about 60 years.

BACK FROM THE BRINK!

Once extinct in the wild, condors are circling the skies of California once more, thanks to an intensive breeding programme.

In 1987, the future looked bleak for the California condor. Conservation workers removed the last six of these vultures from the wild to take part in a last-chance breeding programme.

Five years later, the first condors were released back into the wild. Today, there are wild populations in California and Mexico. The birds are still critically endangered, but their numbers are increasing. They are a conservation success story.

Each condor is given a wing tag and a radio transmitter.

Glossary

captivity Being kept in a cage, unable to escape.

climate change Change in the average weather conditions.

conservation Stopping something (especially the natural environment) from changing or being spoilt.

desert A dry place where little or no rain falls.

drought A long period of dry weather.

endangered In danger of extinction (dying out forever).

extinct Gone forever.

fossil fuel A natural fuel, such as petrol, coal or gas, formed over millions of years from the fossilised remains of living things.

global warming The increase in the temperature of Earth's atmosphere.

greenhouse gas A gas in the Earth's atmosphere that traps heat. Carbon dioxide and methane are both greenhouse gases.

habitat The place where an animal lives.

illegal Against the law; not allowed.

inbreeding Breeding of closely related individuals, which increases the risk of passing on particular health problems.

meteorite strike Hit by a large piece of rock from space.

migrate To make a regular journey, usually to feeding or breeding grounds.

pelt An animal's furry skin.

poacher Someone who takes animals illegally.

pollution Something that makes the air, water or land dirty.

rainforest A thick tropical forest where heavy rain falls every day.

Red List A list of all the animals and plants that are threatened with extinction, published by the IUCN (International Union for Conservation of Nature).

reserve An area of land or sea kept for a special purpose, such as providing a safe place for animals.

species One particular type of living thing. Members of the same species look similar and can reproduce together in the wild.

Further reading and websites

READ MORE ABOUT ENDANGERED ANIMALS:
The Big Countdown: Ten Thousand, Eight Hundred and Twenty Endangered Species in the Animal Kingdom by Paul Rockett (Franklin Watts, 2014)

Eyewitness: Endangered Animals by Ben Hoare and Tom Jackson (Dorling Kindersley, 2010)

Mapping Global Issues: Endangered Species by Peter Littlewood (Franklin Watts, 2011)

READ MORE ABOUT BEING A GREAT WRITER:
How to Write a Story by Simon Cheshire (Bloomsbury, 2014)

How to Write Your Best Story Ever! by Christopher Edge (Oxford University Press, 2015)

The Usborne Write Your Own Story Book (Usborne Publishing, 2011)

DISCOVER MORE ABOUT ENDANGERED ANIMALS ONLINE:
www.greenpeace.org.uk
Greenpeace campaigns to protect oceans, forests and all of the natural world, and to prevent climate change.

wwf.panda.org
WWF International (originally World Wildlife Fund) is one of the world's biggest conservation organisations.

www.wildlifetrusts.org
The UK's Wildlife Trusts campaign to protect wildlife in local areas.

Index